Copywriting

Persuasive Words That Sell

Intro

The aim of this book is to explain to the reader how copywriting can bring countless advantages to sellers.

If you have a business or an e-commerce site, and you want to give a certain boost to sales, a writing job that best reviews the articles you sell is fundamental, especially on the web.

The market has changed, and a good review, perhaps with a strongly persuasive and emotional edge, can make inroads among the readers, bringing them to the purchase.

In this book, therefore, we will focus on defining what copywriting is, what are the most popular techniques for successful writing, the role of SEO copywriting, nowadays essential in the era of the internet and social networks.
We will examine how the persuasive and emotional component plays in the current state of things a role increasingly determined in the eyes of the target audience.

However, the logical, informative, and rational component must never be lacking so that you, as a writer, can be as reliable as possible and not just a salesman.

We will then analyze the barriers that the copywriter has the task of removing, in order to conclude a transaction, what an entrepreneur who hires a copywriter must judge and what are the possible job opportunities for this profession that, unlike many others, does not have a clear and established path, but a myriad of pathways, each distinct from the other.

In the following text, there will be a whole series of useful tips on how to write a heavily sales-oriented text. Enjoy the reading!

Summary

What is copywriting?

In terms of definition, copywriting should be interpreted as the art of knowing how to write well, sometimes informative, sometimes descriptive and, more and more often, as it has been since the boom of advertising, emotional and persuasive.

The target? Ensure conversion. A conversion that, especially in the online world, is represented by the conclusion of a purchase on an e-commerce site, perhaps following the reading of a nice product review written by you, a particularly brilliant copywriter, or a lead that can be subscribing to a newsletter, filling in a contact form and so on.

Each of these goals requires a style of communication that is also appropriate to the type of medium you write about.

Copywriting: origins

The term *copywriting* dates back to the nineteenth century and is specifically related to the journalistic world.

In the editorial offices of most authoritative newspapers, the figure of the copywriter dealt with drawing up all kinds of announcements.

Subsequently, the advertising media boom, first in print and then on radio and TV, totally changed the cards on the table.

In fact, copywriting work was increasingly associated with advertising.

Contributing as a protagonist to the creation of a successful advertising campaign, starting from the creation of slogans to promote the product, were the main work activities for the copywriter, before the advent of the web.

Then, the success of digital marketing has radically changed his duties. So much so that in addition to the professionals who still work in tandem with the art director, who specializes in graphics, there are more and more freelancers covering the multiple textual aspects of the content put online: think for example of the texts for social networks, to corporate blogs where product reviews need to be structured for SEO, so that they are attractive to the various search engines, so that Internet users can find the relevant information.

In short, at present, copywriting is an integral part of internet communication.

Knowing how to communicate the message of a corporate brand, using the right words, the appropriate vocabulary, and the specific SEO oriented writing technique are requirements that only a few possess.

This is why companies are increasingly looking for highly specialized figures in the world of business writing.

And perhaps this research should be based on even more selective criteria, given that unfortunately in an increasingly more competitive market like today, many companies tend to rely on those who ask for lower compensation.

This, as we will explain later, is a huge mistake. There are those who write and those who write well. And to those who write well, merit must always be rewarded, over economic reasoning.

Most effective techniques

Which sales-oriented writing techniques can be considered the best? Giving a straight answer is always complicated.

However, an assumption must be made about the copywriting activity. As a business writer, you have a dual task: to write texts and announcements well that, first of all, must be noticed by the audience of reference.

Secondly, the target you want to return to must appreciate the value of the content you have written. Finally, the company that has chosen you to translate the characteristics of its products into real gains for customers must benefit from your work.

An advantage that has many facets namely increased sales, increased turnover, and growth in the customer base, gains in leads, and more.

Having said that this is a creative job, establishing guidance rules for copywriting is not easy at all.

Therefore we try. Here are the guidelines of the action range in this field.

· Target identification: to whom to communicate? Currently, the message is more and more frequently addressed to the niche.

So, the more specific the niche is, the easier the copywriting text will go.

· The predominant feature of the product must emerge: in a commercial script, the creative, informative, descriptive, technical and persuasive components must never be lacking.

You, a skilled copywriter, have the task of mixing them, arousing emotions and triggering sensations in just a few seconds.

To fully achieve this ambitious goal, you must be able to impress an indelible memory in the minds of readers.

All within a few moments.

The expressions you use in the content must be able to evoke images that no longer go away.

But remember that at the end of the work, what will emerge will be the main feature of the product. The details must be specified within the review, but you must be able to measure them with wisdom because, at the end of the reading, the target you are communicating with will be local and will have to remember first and foremost the fundamental aspect of the product.

This is the so-called principle of formulating a single creative idea, also known as USP (Unique Selling Proposition).

Summing up, based on a specific brief, the most important characteristic decided upstream of the strategy, must come out.

· Zero contradictions: within a text with images or a simple promotional announcement, there is no room for contradictions.

Also because only if you present an excellently structured content, the reading will be as smooth and the decoding will appear simpler. All in full harmony with what the target is looking for.

Having made these clarifications, we review the most common business writing techniques, especially on the web.

Words Consistency

In an SEO oriented text, the keywords must be present in the title of a text, but also in the content of the announcement or article or review. Their use must be measured and the insertion in the text must take place in the most natural way possible, in order to avoid their over-optimization (e.d. known as keyword stuffing) which, inevitably, involves a penalty on search engines.

It is good to combine the keywords with others, most often different, so that the content of the message is strengthened. We will go into this later when we define the principles of SEO Copywriting.

Concreteness in writing style

Whether it is a review or a simple post, the concreteness in the writing style is essential to attract the greatest number of readers, in reference to a product.

Moreover, why should the consumer buy it? As a copywriter, it is up to you to explain it, using a concrete writing style.

Citing numerical data, explaining how to solve a problem, but also using metaphors, because strong images remain in the mind of the reader, they are the key to success in this field.

The Problem Technique

It is a very common copywriting technique, especially concerning tutorials. A question is posed to which many Internet users look for an answer.

Before explaining the solution to the problem, the goal is to involve as many readers as possible. It is important that the question asked should not be rhetorical because if the reader already knows the solution, you seriously run the risk of making every effort vain.

The Alternative technique

Also known as the contrast technique, it is a very widespread scheme when writing with a strong sales orientation.

As an expert in the field, as a copywriter, you can give a question a concrete answer, as a primary solution, and an alternative, always valid. The same is true in the context of online sales.

To suggest the X product as a basic choice for a well-defined target, and the product Y, as a valid option, is a rewarding system.

The important thing is to highlight every single advantage of both primary and secondary choice, but only after having highlighted the characteristics of the two articles. An action of this kind will ensure that you are targeting the target in order to be able to count on more probabilities of satisfying your needs in the best way.

Call to Action

We will discuss the call to action in more depth later on.

For now, we limit ourselves to saying that in the era of the Net, in closing any post, be it a landing page or a review or a commercial ad, the invitation to buy the product, to interact with the brand or signing up for a newsletter is increasingly fashionable.

Only with a highly emotional and persuasive writing technique can the reader be guided towards this step.

Starting from the invitation to action, as we have just highlighted, persuasive copywriting plays a crucial role.

It is not a style of writing suited for everyone since there are precise rules to follow, certain analyzes to be carried out, especially in product reviews, and, above all, to use the appropriate vocabulary.

Target? Persuade the target audience of the goodness of a decision. The starting point of persuasive writing revolves around the analysis of the reader's desires. In fact, it is the needs of the target that move every single action.

The reader must be able to touch the product with the right words. Only if you are a skilled copywriter, will you be able to make every reader see the article reviewed live. A persuasive style of writing must touch emotions.

It is true that sometimes the consumer buys on impulse. However, nowadays, the world has changed: in fact, there are a whole series of categories, such as food and drink, telephony, IT, where customers are very prepared and want to know what they buy, starting from the information they already have.

As a well-traveled business writer, you will need to be able to touch the right ropes.

And to achieve this ambitious and challenging goal, there are rules in the field of persuasive copywriting that is often worth sticking to.

In detail:

Preferring narration to description is the first step that a copywriter must consider when it aims to convince readers of buying a product.

The cancellation of negative sentences must be seen in this sense. "No" and "no" should appear as little as possible.

Eye to the beginning and end of the text: they are the focal points of what you put black on white. Readers on the web initially make a quick read. What matters in any post is the beginning.

It is essential that it is smooth. Only in this way can the attention of the reader be attracted.

The same applies to the lock which must leave something, that is to say, what is special about that product, what distinguishes it from its competitors and why it is worth having. All, of course, before the call to action.

In the middle of the review, regardless of the length, I look at the use of keywords and bold. The attention of the reader is also attracted in this way.

The call to action gives the persuasive cut. Those who read should be guided towards the goal that, as already indicated, can be the purchase of a product, clicking on a link, the insertion of one's own e-mail address for a newsletter. A direct style like an arrow and the impression of an urgent character are the determining factors for making inroads into the hearts of readers.

At the center there are always readers: speaking with their language is the easiest way to reach any goal.

Persuasive copywriting, as we have pointed out, means inducing the potential customer to make the purchase or internet user on duty to perform the classic call-to-action.

However, this does not mean selling at all costs.

A copywriting, whose only imprinting is that of selling, makes reading difficult in the long run, revealing itself to be tiring and in some respects unreliable.

If you use this style of writing, the end result turns out to be in fact counterproductive, since your reliability will be undermined.

Furthermore, the client you work with, be it a company or an e-commerce site, will never benefit from it. So, you'll also be forgoing future collaborations.

Aggressive business writing, whose techniques originate from direct marketing, does not reward in any way.

Little but sure.

Forcing people to take action against the consumer, wanting to capture the attention of those who visit that website, whatever the cost, rather than being an excellent copywriter, they will make you look like a door-to-door salesman (not even very good) also because, with online channels, that contact is missing, that direct approach with the customer that sometimes has the effect due to the conclusion of a transaction.

When writing, therefore, do not think of selling as the number one goal.

Think about what obstacles you need to remove, so that whoever reads you will find it interesting how much you write.

It is no longer as it was in the past, given that, especially thanks to the advent of the Internet, consumers are better prepared and a good slice of purchases, whether these products are at the supermarket, clothes, luxury cars, notebooks, smartphones, tablets, books, gourmet foods are discretionary in nature.

It is therefore impossible to oblige the customer to purchase, regardless of the style of writing that you adopt.
You will be able to induce him to purchase, but you will certainly not be able to force him.

This means that through persuasive copywriting techniques, you will capitalize on a pre-existing need, transforming it into concrete action.

With the emotional cut, you will give to the contents, you will have to create attractiveness towards the described or reviewed products, which the users, especially online, continually seek either because they have a particular problem and intend to solve it or to improve their lifestyle or sometimes for a simple whim.

To induce the customer to purchase, some of the questions you should ask yourself as a business writer are the following: why so many customers have an interest in that product, while others do not even consider them?

What stops the natural inclination to purchase numerous end-users?

Because on a website, many Internet users see different product categories, but then they never go to the cart page?

Basically, there are a whole series of obstacles and impediments that in part, since not everyone has a solution, can be removed with excellent copywriting work.

A persuasive and emotional connotation of editorial content, be it a review or a simple post of advice, can be useful in making the buyer say yes and boost sales.

Your goal as a writer is primarily to identify these barriers that jeopardize the actions of those who read you and then proceed with their elimination.

On the other hand, copywriting is always concerned with sales that tend to rise when there are no objections in the minds of readers.

And it's up to you to wipe them away with messages that leave a measurable impression.

We, therefore, see in a quick overview of what these threats are to be removed.

Identification barrier

Anyone has a personal image that affects their modus operandi. Also during the purchase phase.

As a business writer, when you are reviewing a product, you have to ask yourself if a consumer like you can actually be interested in buying that product. Always ask yourself if what you wrote succeeds in capturing the attention of the reference audience and if the contents can have a connection with the target.

If yes, you worked well and removed the identification barrier. At least this is the first step, to be successful because your words have convinced you.

Clarity barrier

The chances of being able to sell an article to the reader are 0% in the world of copywriting when the latter does not understand what you have written. The savoir-faire, the personal style, the elegance, the good gab, the presence are elements that come out in direct sales. In writing, the contents are important. Make sure the offer is clear. To all. The details of the article must then be understandable above all by the potential target. If what you wrote is clear to you, after a second (or why not, a third and a fourth rereading), it means that you have worked well and that you have removed the barrier of clarity.

Product identity barrier

The product you are writing about must inevitably have a distinctive identity that makes it, in fact, unique compared to the many competitors. After writing the text, try replacing the name of the product in question with that of the most well-known competitor on the market. If the text does not run as smooth as oil, it means that you have worked well, because it has removed the barrier to the identity of the product. Otherwise, if the reading is out of tune, well ... it means that you have not been able to establish the identity of the product and that the end-user, reading your text, will not be able to recognize the actual advantages on why it is worth buying. As a persuasive writer, with an eye to sales, you must have the ability to transform all the main features of the product into advantages for the end customer.

Immediacy barrier

From the first lines, you have to go straight to the point and explain why buying that product is good and urgent. Who reads you must have a clear picture of the benefits of the article. Rewarding those who immediately accept the offer or highlighting that only the last pieces are available from stock is often a winning strategy.

Review the text you have written. If you are convinced that the product is so beautiful to be bought urgently, well then you have worked optimally, because you managed to remove the barrier of immediacy.

Especially in a review, when you write you must appear in the eyes of those who read you credible and reliable. Words give excellent results only if all customer doubts are dispelled.

Especially, however, that there are no miracles in the promotional field.
Using amazing words to pump the product will not have the desired effect.
The quoted testimonials of those who have already tested the product, revealing themselves to be extremely satisfied, is the first step in having a transaction completed.

The same applies to obtaining positive feedback from industry experts. The classic opinion leaders.

If you reread the text, you will be convinced that it is worth buying the product you reviewed, you did a good job and you have removed the reliability barrier

Barrier of involvement

A more immersive reality makes readers and therefore the target audience of the product you are describing more involved.

Inciting their involvement through a check-list or through a quiz is now more and more fashionable, especially on social pages.

It is up to you as a copywriting expert to put the words down to make the offer more attractive. Why is it that today the most is filling in a form or inserting photos, videos, animations, audio?

Simply because they facilitate the activation of the senses.

A well-coordinated work, in this respect, the need for a close collaboration between the copywriter and the art director.

If in the end, the work of which you have been the protagonist seems particularly beautiful to you, it means that you have done an excellent job, because you have removed the barrier of involvement.

Acceptability barrier

The need to be satisfied is to see if the emotional needs you mentioned in the post are particularly in line with those of the target audience. The product must be presented in a very pleasant way. This means that to the persuasive component it is necessary to place side by side of things also the logical, rational one. Only in this way, the text you drafted will not be too commercial.

If you were able to remove the barrier of acceptability, you will only know it over time. Therefore, some factors will prove to be very useful. For example, the entrepreneur you work with will be able to see his audience not as an indistinct and faceless audience, but as a clearly defined target, made up of highly satisfied individuals.

Your readers will see your calls to action particularly meaningfully.

In the long term, those who have worked with you will have long-term contracts with the possibility of repurchase. This means that he will probably want to work with you again, to get you to review more products or maybe he will report you to friends if they specialize in other businesses.

The world of copywriting also relies heavily on word of mouth.

Moreover, in the face of positive results, as a business writer, you will be increasingly able to develop an increasingly realistic approach when you write to sell. And if you're good at that, you might even be able to get around and break the writing rules, creating new ones from scratch.

But this ability is the prerogative of very few. Whiteflies.

The common denominator of these operations of removal of the various barriers consists in fact in being able to package a message tailored to each reader, so that those emotions grow in him that, once they create a concrete need for the product you splendidly reviewed, will induce him to buy it.

SEO Copywriting

On the subject of copywriting, reference has been made to the term SEO. What is the difference between copywriting and SEO copywriting?

Basically, copywriting must be understood as the art of knowing how to structure informative, descriptive contents characterized by a strong emotional and persuasive connotation; SEO copywriting, in addition to the aforementioned criteria, presupposes optimized writing on search engines.

The internet, in fact, offers all businesses, indistinctly, numerous business opportunities. And SEO copywriting allows each company to be found by actual customers and potential customers both on Google and on various search engines. For this to happen, "conditio sine qua non" is the writing of authoritative, interesting, useful and pertinent texts with Internet users' searches. All SEO oriented.

From an SEO copywriting perspective, metadata should be used in a workmanlike manner. The same applies to the structuring of the contents. The keywords must be inserted in the title and present in the text. Only in this way, indexing will be at the highest levels. In commercial writing, more web-oriented, for an article to be attractive to search engines, H1, H2, meta description, and keywords should be used with criteria.

The more the SEO rules, which we will shortly indicate, will be respected, the higher the ranking of the text on search engines. And for a company, this translates into a considerable advantage.

Three e-commerce sites sell that food processor that is so popular in recent times. One has only the description of the product, the other a simple review and, finally, the last one optimized on the web with an indication of the strengths and testimonies of those who bought the item and was highly satisfied.

What do you think has the best chance of appearing on the first page of Google? Clearly, the last one, can't you find it too?

In the face of large numbers, in the world of e-commerce, sell that product that appears on the first page of Google in a natural way. when the Internet users search for it by inserting only its name in the query, well... it is a very significant competitive advantage, as the company increases sales, collects money, frees up space in the warehouse and benefits in terms of turnover.

Do you understand that the role of primary importance must be attributed to SEO copywriting?

So here are the most relevant rules in the production of content on the web that a good SEO copywriter must take into consideration.

SEO Techniques

Title tags, meta descriptions, header tags, URLs, and text must be optimized for search engines. This is possible only when, as a copywriter, you know the rules and secrets of business writing on the web in detail, Therefore ...

Title Tag

Of all the SEO factors, the Title tag is by far the most decisive. The title keyword must be placed at the beginning, next to the site name. The only exception to this rule is only the homepage, where the brand name must have the right relevance, just as if it were the keyword. For the other web pages, it becomes crucial to insert the relevant keywords in a meaningful way: the name of the brand, however, should not be included at all. The reason for this strategy is that following the keyword with the brand name results in a reduction in the importance given by the title tag to the associated keyword.

Another gross error to keep clear of is the insertion of excess text within the title tag.

Its greater length corresponds to a clear division of the importance assigned to the different keywords in the text.

Meta description

It should always be valued, as it must best describe the web page that the visitor is about to read. Also in this, the call to action that invites you to click right there is very useful, unlike doing so on one of the other available results. In this way, the company that operates in e-commerce has the possibility of achieving one of the many objectives already mentioned several times. Although among these, the sale of a product is almost always the most important.

Header tags

Use in the text h1, h2, h3 tags. It is vitally important to make the reading more fluent: the header tags ensure that the paragraphs are not excessively long and that the information is not presented, in terms of character, in a flattened manner. Adopting header tags, especially for the content of a certain length, is a wise decision. In relation to the rules for writing header tags, we immediately tell you that there are no definite ones. Their usefulness is to give a title to the paragraph or to the reference paragraph below.

Url Keyword Rich

Containing keywords is one of the essential requirements of web page URLs, given the importance that the Mountain View Colossus search engine attaches to this aspect. The keywords, and especially the primary one, must be present in the URL which, in turn, must be exploited precisely to give them considerable visibility. In this way, the positioning of the page will be even more natural.

Paragraphs

SEO copywriting has undergone an important change in recent years. Writing an over-optimized text from an SEO point of view, until a few years ago, allowed you to have more visibility on the web than the competition, for what concerns the use of those specific keywords. The result, however, is that this excessive optimization annoyed and not a little the Internet users.

Today, this principle has changed. When writing, the text must be designed not for the search engine, but for the reader.
Knowing how to enhance the title tag, meta description, header tags, and paragraphs are the key to getting the right visibility online.

What about text and paragraphs at this point?

The text must respond perfectly to the title tag and the description so that the reader does not be disappointed when accessing the web page from Google's SERP.

In the absence of this assumption, as a copywriter, you will not be clearly writing for the reader, but for the search engine.

And on this point, it is good that you immediately realize it when you start writing. The reason? The satisfaction of the reader is at the moment the main point that Google takes into consideration. On this aspect, especially in recent years, progress has been truly remarkable. The merit must be assigned to updates to qualitative algorithms that return web pages to the internet user, more and more in line with her research questions. Basically, all those websites and web pages that best respond to the queries of those who surf the web are the winners.

The long form

Recently, one of the most popular topics in the field of copywriting is certainly the long form, also known as pillar article. What is it essentially? Specifically, it is a text rich in content that in some respects closely resembles a mini tutorial.

Have you ever tried to search on Google for "How to ..." and to find a mini guide, where you had to click on "Next" to view the individual steps from time to time?

Well, the long form is this but without the annoying chopping of the text into multiple pages.

A mini tutorial that fits into a single web page with the individual passages enumerated, one after the other. This is very widespread in the field of sales-oriented writing, but also in the field of IT-oriented websites or in generalist news blogs or in editorial magazines.

Ultimately, the underlying mission of the long form is to give you an excellent opportunity, namely to create a whole series of web pages that are positioned on the various search engines based on specific keywords. All without having to insert external links.

There is no ideal length that allows you to classify that text as a long form. However, the minimum presence of 2,500 words and 3 or 4 paragraphs is a prerequisite for developing a specific topic in depth. Each long form revolves around a central keyword and several secondary keywords.

Using an index in HTML format, to be placed under the title is a wise choice for a good construction of a long form of art. The underlying reason for this strategic choice, in fact, is to present in a concise way, through an easy navigation path, which points are analyzed in the mini guide, thus giving the reader immediately the possibility of knowing where to find the solution to his question.

Keyword research

In reference to business writing on the web, the topic of SEO copywriting represents the decisive phase, as the actual research intent, the various synonyms of the main keyword that Internet users could type online, all the features that present a association with the keyword, ie price, recipient, destination and, finally, all the relevant adverbs: how, where, how, when, why and so on. In this phase, as a copywriter, the search query expansion method will be decisive.

The structure to be followed will, in fact, be of a pyramid type: the keyword placed at the top followed in rapid succession by secondary keywords based on the greater volume of traffic and all the semantic links that the internet user could type on the search engine.

Fortunately, in this process, you will be able to count on various tools that the world of the web puts at your disposal: Google Keyword Planner, Google Suggest, AnswerthePublic, and Keyword Magic Tool are certainly the most competitive. The common denominator of these tools is the precise work focused primarily on the analysis of the primary keywords and only subsequently on the levels of competition and traffic volumes.

And in reference to the content to be structured, be it an article or a mini guide, what do you have to do as a sales-oriented commercial writer?

The keyword must be the basis of the article and is present in every paragraph, subparagraph and under the title.

This means that you will need to use the largest possible number of variables in an organic and logical way so that Internet users will find your content on search engines on one side and readers on the other hand to consider the article relevant to their query.

Conclusions

Here, therefore, are the tricks to keep in mind in the context of SEO copywriting.

· For the title, it is preferable to opt for the h1 tag

· For paragraphs, it is wise to adopt the h2 tag

· For the subparagraphs, it is good to prefer the use of the h3 tag

· The keywords must be used in the most natural way possible, but in a manner consistent with what the title of the article and its contents indicate

· In order to avoid over-optimization, due to the continuous use of the same keywords, dosing the variables wisely makes the texts even better structured: singular, plural and synonyms of the keyword are always welcome

· Bold and italics are very useful because they make the reading smoother. Moreover, since the contents immediately jump to the sight of the visitors, they have the possibility to find as soon as possible the information pertinent to their search

· Bulleted lists and numbered lists make the reading smoother

· In order for a text to be optimized on search engines, Google in the first place, with an ideal minimum length is 300 words

· Using internal links and external links is an excellent strategy: the important thing is that all the sources highlighted are consistent with the argument, authoritative as sources and useful to those who surf the Internet. The links must always be inserted on the anchor text of certain relevance.

· The use of meta tags is indispensable so that Google and other search engines consider the text to be of a certain level

· The images eventually inserted in the text must be named using the keywords adopted in the contents. If in the event there were alternative fields, also, in this case, it is necessary to compile them. Particularly eye to the meta description. This is essentially the summary of what was written. It is important that the keywords, even in this situation, are always present.

Online Tools

If you want to do SEO Copywriting in Italian, there are a whole series of online tools available on the Net that can be extremely useful. These are basically tools that do textual analysis but not only. In this paragraph, we will present them one by one in rapid tracking, in relation to what appears to be their primary function.

1. Identification of sources and definition of ideas: the creative process

This is the first phase of SEO Copywriting, where the work is basically scouting. Reason for which the consultation of the sources, aimed at identifying the statistics, the various points of view and the relevant case studies, is of primary importance for the definition of ideas, for the creation of the text and for the enrichment of contents. Two of the most competitive tools of all are Pocket (www.getpocket.com) and Feedly (www.feedly.com).

- Pocket: what it is and how it works

What is Pocket? In a nutshell, this is a valid online application to save articles to read them more calmly at a later time and to have all your interests at hand. Specifically, this content care tool allows you to start working on the right foot, since you can order ideas sensibly, critically evaluate selected cues and decide which ones to discard and which ones to use and then share them later. Pocket is one of the most successful tools in the field of SEO Copywriting due to its considerable practicality: first of all, it ensures that you do not miss the links of all the articles, photos, and videos you wish to consult later. In this way, in fact, the organization and productivity of your work will benefit.

The Pocket operation logic is simple and intuitive: once on the homepage, all you have to do is create an account by registering via e-mail or via Google. After that, the immediate saving of articles, images, and videos will be a breeze, since you can count on the appropriate button or on the Google Chrome bookmarklet, Safari, Firefox. Once you have selected the posts that you consider most noteworthy, these will be added to your personal list. Alternatively, Pocket offers you the possibility to insert the links also from within the application or in the web page called Save an item to Pocket. The possibility of tagging your links in the way that suits you best is really very convenient since you will have a better organization from your side. The internal search, in this regard, allows you to more easily find the contents that, depending on your actual needs, can also have multiple tags. All editable and removable, of course. The Untagged items item is very useful because it allows you to consult all those contents, which were saved without inserting any tag.

Clearly, advanced features are not lacking. The links that have impressed you the most can be placed in the favorites, with the star mark. If you consider it appropriate, you can also put them in the archived (editor's note: Archive). Excellent Text to Speech (TTS) function that reads the article of interest in the language you set. In this way, you will be able to listen and collect the idea while you are busy with other matters.

The beauty of Pocket is that it works perfectly even off-line since the contents can be read even when you are not connected.

The same applies to read at a later time: in this case, you can select one of the two available fonts, enlarge or reduce the font and select one of the three colors for the layout. All the contents saved, therefore, with Pocket can be consulted even without being online. Connection, on the other hand, is an essential requirement for sharing content on social networks, such as Facebook and Twitter or via e-mail. In this last example, the item to be selected is Send to a friend: the recipient will see the link not only in his e-mail box but, if he is a registered user, also in the Inbox of this very valid web-based service, clean in the interface and extremely user-friendly in terms of use.

Also for Recommendations, internet connection is essential. The beauty of Pocket is that over time it starts to know what your actual preferences are and to suggest which content is most relevant to you. In fact, when you write, you will lose less and less time in selecting sources. The most interesting ones, you can easily collect them in the Recommended section. The last thing to be specified about Recommendations is that you can save and tag content that is worth reading to you. Then it will clearly be up to you to decide whether to take inspiration from these sources in the sales-oriented online writing phase.

Another first-order advantage in using Pocket lies in teamwork. Still, with the Send to a Friend function, you can insert content into the interface of the online application and send an e-mail message to add@getpocket.com. The contents entered will be sent to the list you have created. By adding the e-mail addresses of your team members from your personal profile options, you can easily work in groups, even remotely.

Summing up, Pocket is really the non-plus ultra if you constantly look for ideas for your content and you don't always have time available for screening the sources. Ditto if you can't read on the fly. How many times you're having a look at the social pages or your favorite internet sites, did you happen to find really interesting contents, but that in that specific moment you could not consult? Well, Pocket solves your problem.

- Feedly: what it is and how it works

In the SEO copywriting branch, Feedly turns out to be a high-level tool, for the simple reason that it allows you to increase your knowledge and identify the essential points to share relevant topics, especially in the field of social media marketing and blogging. Select the sources with the utmost care: this is essentially the basic function of the aforementioned online service, in order to improve your work. The moment you consult content posted by other users and intend to use it, Feedly lets you name them or more precisely to address your sources with extreme precision. One of the most used systems in the field of source selection is the organization of content by project, where it focuses on customers. Specifically, each directory constitutes a project that contains the most suitable sources for the creation of new texts. Idem for the organization of content by theme, where folders are used to synthesize the themes for the development of a single project.

But the functions of this valuable resource certainly do not end here. Feedly turns out to be an excellent feed reader that, among other things, is one of the most appreciated by bloggers. The distinctive feature of this online service lies in the fact that thanks to RSS feeds it is not necessary to constantly follow your favorite blogs. The contents can be read easily in the feed reader.

Another interesting aspect of Feedly is the possibility of adding a blog. All you have to do is search from the appropriate bar or type in the URL and press enter. From the added blog box, you will see the preview of the last posted content. By clicking on the green cross, you will have completed the operations. The strength of Feedly lies in the possibility of defining in the read which content to publish on social networks and what to highlight later. For every post published on Feedly, there are a whole series of valid blogging tools. This is also very useful for sales-oriented writing. As a business writer, in fact, you can highlight an interesting article for a project. If you then want to go deeper into it, perhaps to rework it, you can save it in the Saved for the later folder. For sharing on social networks, nowadays more and more important to increase traffic on your client's website and, consequently, to give an impulse to his sales, if he also did e-commerce, you can take advantage of all the functions on the right side of the menu. The same is true for sending content to your contacts through an e-mail message. However, these functions are only available in the version of Feedly Pro (https://feedly.com/i/pro), the price currently amounts to 5.41 dollars a month.

So, to sum up, choosing Feedly as a working tool in the business writer branch is very practical both for a speech organizing discovery of the sources. To inform you, in fact, the content worthy of note we will think this valid online service. After registering for a blog, suggestions will be made automatically, even taking into account the interests that your contacts share. The merit of this opportunity lies rightly with the tags inserted in the feed. Suffice it to think that under each title there is a variety of information available, from the contents that are reported to you and that you must still read to the readers who have subscribed to the feed, without forgetting the tags, whose basic mission consists both in the suggestions blog but also in navigation between the contents.

Finally, Feedly also has the Shared Collection from her that will make you an influencer copywriter. You can tell users what you read. Consequently, they will decide whether to follow what is suggested. Such as? Via the RSS Feed button: once the address has been entered, select the key that best suits you based on the size, and indicate to the readers which updates are the most worthy of attention.

In terms of customer loyalty, what's better than this tool?

2. Keyword definition

Defining keywords and their synonyms is part of the SEO Copywriting work that should always be done upstream. There are really many useful tools in this regard. Google Ads is certainly the best known, but certainly not the only one.

- Google Ads and basic suggestions for creating a list of keywords

Known as Google Adwords until July 24, 2018, this online advertising service, created by the Colossus of Mountain View, is undoubtedly the most complete for inserting advertising spaces in the search pages. Of course, Google. The job of the

SEO copywriter is to select the best list of keywords in relation to the reference advertising campaign. Doing a good job, in this sense, allows you to show Internet users, who are always potential customers, the ads most relevant to their search questions. The keywords, in this respect, must always correspond to the terms used by those browsing on Google to search for items that the customer you work for sells. Finding this keyword list on the fly is certainly not easy. For this reason, flexibility is essential for you, as you must always be ready to enter new keywords and, if necessary, change them or even remove some.

The main advice we feel we can give you is to always identify with the Internet users. Write down the core business categories of the business you are collaborating with, select the most common terms, opt for the phrases that best describe the categories is very useful to search more easily. For example, you are a copywriter who works with a company that specializes in selling sports shoes. Very well. At the classic query MEN'S SPORTS SHOES, you could add two more, like MEN'S GYMNASTICS SHOES or MEN'S RACING SHOES. After that, evaluate the trend. Are these terms used as often as Internet users access your partner's website? If the answer is negative, as we

94

have already stated, you need to modify the list of keywords and maybe go to WINTER SPORTS SHOES or SUMMER TENNIS SHOES. If, on the other hand, the work defined above proceeds at full speed, you can associate the previously used name with the name of the trademark of men's sneakers or men's running shoes.

To approach specific customers, the list of keywords must also be as specific as possible. Always naturally connected to the theme of the online advertisement you are about to make. Not making this job upstream is a pretty serious mistake, because you would go to lose a whole series of potential customers, perhaps even particularly profitable ones.

Still remaining anchored to the previous example, choosing as a specific word MEN'S RUNNING SHOES, you can count on an announcement that will be shown to all internet users looking for this type of sports shoes.

Also in this type of work is the interception of a specific niche that determines success.

However, as an SEO Copywriter, you should always try to reach as many users as possible, starting with specific keywords. In fact, starting with too general words does not pay, because the road to reach those who surf the internet becomes more tortuous.

The competition is getting higher and higher and you would end up squandering the budget that the company in charge puts at your disposal, given that the offer inevitably tends to rise. Experimentation, in this case, as already pointed out, is the characteristic that must never be lacking in this work.

To find the best keyword list, you need to test the results in the field.

It is good, however, to avoid the use of duplicate keywords within your account in any way possible.

Why? Well, Google shows you a single ad per advertiser, referring to a specific keyword.

Choosing SHOES as a keyword is too general, although maybe you could reach a user looking for a pair of shoes. The problem is that you would end up paying a lot for an announcement and not to conclude anything if the person concerned doesn't make any transaction. Better to opt for example on FASHION GYMNASTIC SHOES.

An excellent strategy is that of grouping similar keywords within ad groups. When you work with Google Ads, give online surfers the chance to display more relevant ads in relation to the items of interest, it's a goal you never have to move away from, for example, create two groups of advertisements, such as DA GINNASTICA DA MAN and MEN'S EVENING SHOES. To this second group, add variables, such as ELEGANT MEN'S SHOES, CLASSIC MEN'S SHOES, MEN'S LEATHER SHOES.

This division will ensure that men's evening shoes are displayed by Internet users only when they type the last three queries and not in the case of MEN'S GYMNASTICS SHOES.

What to say finally about the number of keywords? Is there a right number of keywords for a single group of advertisements? It is not a fixed rule, but the ideal number is between a minimum of 5 and a maximum of 20.

It is preferable that each individual ad group contains the keywords directly related to the underlying theme of the group.

The variants, as singular and plural (editor's note not the case for shoes, but maybe for jacket/jackets, coat/coats) will be included automatically and there is no need to add them.

The same applies to any spelling or typing errors that can occur when the user conducts his search query.

- Ubersuggest: an essential tool to improve your blogging and SEO Copywriting activity

In the toolbox of essential SEO tools in the world of online copywriters, one of the most interesting tools in the Keyword Planner landscape is Ubersuggest (https://neilpatel.com/ubersuggest/). What is it? Of an SEO tool, developed by Neil Patel, with the aim of guaranteeing the advantageous opportunity to search for the most relevant keywords, as an expert in the field of search engine optimization.

If you are also a blogger, Ubersuggest also offers you the most interesting topics for your projects. Its operation is very simple since it organizes as a list of all the suggestions that Google has indicated in the field of queries typed by users:

At the base of everything, whether you are a particularly active copywriter in the production of commercial content or a successful blogger, there is the drafting of quality contents that intercept the needs of those who surf the web. Answer the question But what are people looking for? it is the first determining factor to obtain or to obtain good results. And Ubersuggest sets itself precisely in this context: directly from the homepage, all you have to do is fill in the three aforementioned fields: keyword, source, and language. To refine the results, it is a wise choice to include in the sources what you really care about, namely shopping or the web for purely commercial or Youtube aspects, news and images for issues related instead to issues from non-profit bloggers. Below, you will always see the result with a summary of the data relating to a given keyword taken into consideration.

What makes Ubersuggest truly unique, however, is that it provides you with a wealth of useful information, from search volumes to keyword competition, without forgetting the cost per click. The reference section also allows you to view the results of Google Suggest and Keyword Planner which, if deemed appropriate, you can also filter. Two other filters are also excellent on the keywords you need and on the negative ones to remove.

At a strategic level, Ubersuggest plays a role of primary importance in SEO Copywriting, as it allows you to find the most useful keywords for your purposes, to improve Google meta tags and to present optimized content, especially on corporate blogs.

Much of the work with this tool is oriented to an analytical study of the queries made by users on the main search engines: in this way, it is much easier to identify the target with the personas. How to achieve this goal? Query Ubersuggest, depending on the topic for which you are of particular interest. Carefully examine the results and, in order to be more precise, do not take into consideration the results of the Keyword Suggest, as it is sometimes excessively dispersive as a channel. Within this list of results, what you need to carefully evaluate are the questions, shared needs and needs associated with various lifestyles. You should, in fact, start to take advantage of the selection within the boxes of every single keyword, in order to have only the bare essentials at hand. This material will obviously have to be seriously considered in your editorial plan.

But Ubersuggest does much more since it allows you to learn about new titles, useful for your writing job: you can dissect a topic at 360 degrees, perhaps starting from general encyclopedic content and then continuing with the pillar articles, definitely more specific, and with longtail articles, connected to a specific deepening.

As for the writing of the post that you will re-elaborate from other sources, based on the suggested keywords, the use of H2 is essential to intercept the needs of the target you intend to approach so that your attention is captured as quickly as possible.

Even the search for secondary keywords and keywords related to the central topic is indispensable and Ubersuggest, never as in this case, turns out to be a valuable ally. Ditto for the more complex branches, where the presence of H3 and H4 is a "sine qua non" condition for the presentation of highly structured content. If you also need a resource to present a summary or a conceptual map to accompany the text, especially in the case of longer sales-oriented articles, a resource like Coggle (https://coggle.it/) is really the non-plus ultra, due to the ease with which it allows you to represent complex ideas, even via Flow Charts.

Finally, if you want to learn more about how to find secondary keywords, which variants match the main keyword, how to expand the semantic field of the central topic and how to improve the writing of content to be published online, always but not only in terms of commercial writing, well... Ubersuggest is just right for you.

3. Online writing

Having already clear what kind of content to structure, the cut to be given to the post (emotional/persuasive or informative/rational, formal or informal), how the content list should be structured, it is good to consider what tool can do to the case yours for what concerns online writing. Hemingway Editor (http://www.hemingwayapp.com/) is one of the most credible alternatives to the classic Word sheet or to the CMS platform of the website where you are going to publish your ideas. The more you put down text, the longer you will be able to view various parameters, flanked by a whole series of highlights, worthy of a reflection without a doubt. Among these, it is worth mentioning the number of words (counting), the level of legibility of the content (feedback), the length of the sentences, the complexity of the periods, the repetitiveness of the words (excellent reporting of synonyms and variants), the judgment on the use of bold, italics, insertion of hyperlinks and citations (essential in the fast reading phase on the web).

4. The control of the texts

Before publishing a text online, especially if you have consulted a considerable number of sources, it is worth carrying out an accurate check. Control is a word that indicates various monitoring operations of how much you've actually knocked out.

The reason why:

- In reference to the synonyms and opposites, as well as the use of words, anagrams, definitions, and citations, Dizy (https://www.dizy.com/) is one of the most reliable services ever. A dictionary containing useful information and curiosities, which really deserves to be consulted several times during the drafting of the post. For synonyms and antonyms, also Synonyms - Antonyms of the Italian language (https://www.sinonimi-contrari.it/) is an excellent source, as there are few on the web.

- As regards the repetitiveness of the words used in the text you wrote, excellent online service is certainly Repetition Detector 2 (http://www.repetition-detector.com/), whose primary purpose revolves around the Highlighting of excessively used words. In terms of SEO Copywriting, given the reporting of synonyms, its use is essential to avoid repetitiveness and give more verve to the reader.

- As part of Copyscape, Plagium (https://www.plagium.com/) is one of the easiest web-based services to use. Clean in design and spartan in the interface this valid plagiarism detection tool gives you the opportunity to check if other authors have used the same words to explain to readers or to promote products in the form of reviews. Copy and paste the text (up to 5,000 characters, but you can also make more queries) in the appropriate internal search engine and click on Quick Search or Deep Search, depending on whether you prefer a quick or deeper scan. If some source is too equal to what you wrote, Plagium will show you the text too similar and the percentage of words already used.

Then it's up to you to replace them and rework the sentences.

5. The re-reading of the text

It has already been argued that syntax errors, as well as spelling errors, undermine the reliability of the content and seriously jeopardize the authority of the writer. In the case of a sales-oriented SEO Copywriting work, the company is the first to lose. Therefore, the re-reading of the text is essential.

Which web-based tools can help you?

Free Online Spell Checker (https://www.jspell.com/public-spell-checker.html), as well as Language Tool Proofreading Service (https://www.languagetool.org/it/), are two excellent tools in the reporting of misprints

Using them is the right decision. Their operation is as intuitive as it is since it is sufficient to copy and paste what you have already written and wait for the necessary time so that these web-based services give you the results.

Learn copywriting

Knowing how to write well in Italian, to respect the grammatical rules, to know the use of punctuation at best are essential requisites for becoming a successful copywriter.

But they are not enough alone.

Unlike other paths more or less related to the world of writing, from the teacher to the journalist, from the lawyer to the notary, along the same lines as for successful writers, even in the case of copywriters the path is not so linear.

This profession can develop into many branches. The basics are different for everyone.

What we want to tell you is that a degree in the humanities, an internship in an advertising agency, having already written for newspapers, owning a blog even with many visitors, a specialization course in creative or persuasive writing (we will soon deepen even better this point) as much as they help, not only are they not indispensable, but sometimes they are not decisive. Always following this logic, having just one or all the requirements listed above will not automatically make you a successful copywriter.

Useful suggestion for writing high-quality content is the registration with thematic groups on Facebook or on LinkedIn. Here, in fact, you will be able to read a whole series of useful opinions on both sales-oriented copywriting and on creative writing, as well as on everything that revolves around the creation of an advertising campaign that has obtained the consent of the relevant public.

It is then appropriate to specialize in selected topics and it is better if these coincide with one's passions.

Moreover, it is nowadays the conquest of a niche that decrees the success on the market. And a happy and satisfied professional makes a lot more in terms of work. And commercial writing is certainly not an exception to these rules. Acting in this way, the possibility of coming into contact with companies that want to associate their brand with your writing style for the production of creative content or persuasive texts will be greater. Little but sure.

And on this aspect, having a blog can be very useful, as companies can contact you more easily.

The important thing is to produce creative, stylish, unique content on the Web, but in a constant manner.

Writing one-time or so for ... well it won't give you any noteworthy results.

Returning to the talk about the courses to follow, there are plenty of them and many of them are also online. Follow them is an extra opportunity that, especially if you are at the beginning in this sector, will allow you to stand out from the competition because you will be able to learn the secrets of the best experts in the sector. The difference, however, is made by the desire to learn, the style of writing, having creative skills and being able to adapt, given that customer requests will always be the most varied and propose the tone of voice for the target of reference is not always easy.

Who is the skilled copywriter?

A versatile thinker who knows the language in depth, knowing how to express it with mastery over a specific channel, be it the paper, the web or other media. Just like a seasoned seducer, the writer must influence, fascinate and conquer each individual with a text.

At the same time, this communication expert can be considered as a real architect of the text, an artist of words or even a curious creative who for the whole day has to do with texts, titles, slogans, naming , headline, word games and that perhaps constantly strives to transform into words the strategies of a company or the concept of a specific brand.

Regardless of the type of product, its basic mission always remains to make users call for action.

But let's proceed with the order.

In modern marketing, sales-oriented writing is essential for a company that decides to market products.

More and more companies are entrusting the copywriter with the task of writing reviews and texts to adapt nowadays mainly to the web, but also slogans for TV and radio, as well as texts for billboards and for press announcements. For copywriting jobs, entrepreneurs mostly prefer to work with advertising agencies. In fact, the copywriter increasingly works in the agency. Only a few companies prefer to have this figure within the staff.

Moreover, more and more copywriters work as freelancers. In Italy, however, less than in many European countries.

The successful copywriter is one who has creative talent, who knows how to experiment and who always has straight antennas... Doing more than a successful job that favors the increase in sales in a company, unlike in the past, may not even be enough.

The reason? The market is constantly changing, and a certain modus operandi, specific techniques for producing sales-oriented texts do not necessarily mean that they last outside.

Even in the field of commercial writing, reiterating the same model to infinity does not work.

Dropping the antennas means always considering alternative ways to effectively communicate to customers, whether actual or potential, the value of the products promoted. All even when the sales trend is positive. Knowing how to experiment is one of the many factors of success in commercial writing because it allows you to sell in an alternative way.

The work of the copywriter

Both large companies and small and medium-sized companies, as well as start-ups, are looking for specialized figures in the field of copywriting, especially in the SEO branch.

Putting high-quality content online is the easiest way to be appreciated in the eyes of customers who deserve to read well-structured texts. More and more often, in this regard, you may have read the maxim "Content is King."

The real motivation is that in the era of social networks, where interactions are social in nature, sharing high-quality content is an important advantage for a company since there is not only money at stake, but also market share, competitive advantage, and brand popularity.

To achieve success in the eyes of staff recruiters, the creative qualities, the style of writing with a high persuasive and emotional impact, the experiences gained on the right and on the left are an added value.

But also the transversal competencies, that is to say to be able to range in the SEO branch, in the field of visual communication or in advertising, where it is necessary to highlight the product's strengths, nevertheless represent a point in your favor, in the moment in you wish to apply for this job.

In recent times, the selection of copywriters has definitely increased, because companies aim to communicate the right content as precisely as possible. Also because then it is the company brand that benefits.

The latter, when it can count on well-written content, has the opportunity to create contact with potential customers. What we, therefore, want to tell you that in Italy, despite the crisis, there is certainly no lack of offers in the copywriting sector. And the same argument is also valid at the world level. Therefore, if you have a perfect knowledge of English or any other foreign language and writing is one of your many passions, all you have to do is enhance your creative talent, putting yourself to the test in this area.

In terms of job opportunities, regardless of the type of communication in which he works, if he works in an advertising agency, the figure of the copywriter is almost always internalized.

It is normal for an agency worthy of the name to have a series of projects every month.

And the good copywriter will have to follow various projects.

It is, therefore, a work that goes well beyond the canonical 8 hours. Advertising agencies and consulting companies, in fact, do not know timetables. Try searching through job listings. In Italy and especially in Milan, the figure of the copywriter is increasingly sought after.

In an advertising agency, if the working collaboration concerns companies of a certain thickness, given the institutional cut and the formal communication, the monthly salary of a copywriter can exceed 2,000 euros. Then clearly, the pay varies from the projects you follow.

But there is not only the advertising agency among the job opportunities of the aforementioned professional figure. Even if it is an alternative to the web agency or the classic media agency, there are several companies that prefer to have a copywriter on their staff. The problem, however, is that generally, this professional does everything in the branch of marketing and communication. It does not deal only with sales-oriented writing, aimed at enhancing the company's products or corporate brand, but also takes care of communication on social networks, writes tests on the company blog, defines the communication strategy on off-line channels, deals with customer assistance, draws up the marketing operational plan in collaboration and much more. On this point, in this regard, many companies should have clearer ideas.

However, more and more copywriters decide to start their own business working as a freelance.

As freelancers, they, in fact, have a VAT number, a very welcome requirement for companies. The main reason is that copywriting is a work that revolves around specific projects and not a continuous collaboration, day by day. Unless, as we have already had to highlight, that of the copywriter is not a figure internalized by companies and web agencies.

So, if on the one hand there are entrepreneurial realities who prefer to work on projects, giving the copywriter, as an external collaborator, the possibility of achieving a specific goal, on the other hand there is to say that there are media agencies or companies that, having understood the potential of digital well in advance, they prefer to have in the staff a figure totally dedicated to the care of communication at 360 degrees.

In any case, as a matter of flexibility, in the current state of affairs, many prefer the freelance solution, given that the work is organized and managed independently. If you are a freelancer in the field of commercial writing, you will certainly know that time and money. So, the clearer the directives, the less you will need to interface with the company on duty, since you have a perfect overview of the projects to follow, the more you will earn at the economic level. Time is money, never like in this field.

Conclusions

At this point, you will certainly have a clearer overview of the field of copywriting. In reference to how to start, as we have already anticipated, a training course, fundamental for learning the basics in the various branches of this discipline, can be the turning point for you.

Listening to the experience of authoritative experts on the subject is the first step to create your own toolbox and to know where to act and how to intervene. The reading of concrete case studies and the experimentation in writing sales-oriented texts with an emotional slant is for many the launch pad in this new sector.

Are you ready to accept this exciting challenge?

Copy for business

Copywriting to sell

Writing to sell, in the era of e-commerce and social networks, has become a job in every respect.

Do you have any idea how many companies have put really excellent products on the market, often revolutionary, but which, unfortunately, are not successful, because the message conveyed does not have the desired effect, influencing the target audience?

139

Like it or not, companies that are unable to communicate what they produce almost never succeed in sales.

In a nutshell, entrepreneurial and managerial talent is essential to market high value and exquisite workmanship products, but without copywriting, sales feedback will not be up to par.

In order to avoid that the product you are going to put on the market does not obtain the desired success, as an entrepreneur, you cannot do without commercial copy, able to best present to the customer what you are selling.

What is the job of a good copywriter?

Highlight the strengths of the product and bring out its distinctive features.

Those that, for instance, ensure your company competitive advantage. On the basis of a strategy agreed upstream between the company and the copywriter, the message conveyed may be informative, professional, descriptive or, as it happens more and more often, a more emotional one. At the decision-making level, the type of product put on the market will have an influence that is certainly not trivial.

If your company, with the support of a well-planned and efficient copywriting strategy, is able to better communicate commercial messages, it will have the opportunity to be able to increase, and even drastically, sales. All regardless of the channel used for the dissemination of promotional messages, whether off-line or online. Good writing always gives the core business of your business a little something extra.

Being able to have in your staff copywriters able to make the best use of the rules of good sales-oriented writing, makes your company make a remarkable leap in quality.

How to write to sell?
Returning to the question that is the subject of this paragraph, here are some useful tips

to fully achieve your goals, as an entrepreneur.

Who should you contact?

To ensure a turnaround in your business and to boost your sales, the choice of a commercial copywriter is a decisive factor. Which business writer do you have to choose to promote the products you sell? The evaluation process that leads you to the final decision should not be absolutely underestimated.

There are many entrepreneurs who prefer to save on the budget because they mistakenly think that all business writers are able to write. This is the wrong choice because only a few know how to have a sales-oriented writing cut. The recruitment of a professional with proven experience, who has already reviewed products in the same sector in which your company moves and which has brought serious results to those who have requested its services, is fundamental to increase your turnover and your company popularity, as well as to bring the product to a leading role in the market.

Writing well and communicating effectively

The creation of an advertising type message (advertising note, to be understood as making the product values public) is the primary purpose of copywriting directed to the sale. From the indefinite audience of the recipients of the message, there is the target audience, composed of potential customers. Those that potentially have an interest in the product. The writing of the skilled copywriter must be targeted to this slice of the audience. To achieve the goal, the good copywriter must start putting himself in the shoes of the product target, foreseeing what his actual needs are. How does the relevant public act? What needs do customers have to buy this product? What are consumer habits? How do decisions are made during the purchase phase? What is the spring that then opens the wallet? Only by reasoning with the head of the target (and this is not easy), the writer will allow your company to intercept the concrete needs of the demand.

A direct style helps and not a little in the field of sales. And this is even more true for the writer. The reason? Those who read the messages often do not have much time. Moreover, in an era where you are constantly bombarded with promotional messages, the copywriting text must be distinctive. The readers and the target will not give infinite credit to your business. Indeed, it is exactly the opposite. The credit your company must take care of. And even in the shortest possible time. Based on the above, an excellent copywriting work revolves around resorting to the minimum of words, so that the greatest possible amount of information is conveyed in the message conveyed to the target audience. All of course of quality, in order to best describe the specifications of the product put on the market. Going straight to the heart of the matter, using a direct style, in fact, also rewards in terms of sales.

Bring value to your target

A winning copywriter is one who knows how to create value for the target, affecting the selective attention of potential customers. How to fascinate customers, capturing their interest? Valuing product benefits, explaining why it is necessary to have one, or guiding those directly involved in solving a problem step by step are two of the main keys to the success of an effective message. In the commercial field, transmitting value to customers allows your company to have important economic returns thanks to the written word.

Reliability?

When you rely on a copywriter to advertise your product, you must be informed in detail about his writing style. The first question you have to ask is whether it is reliable. Even in sales-oriented copywriting, reliability and authority are two fundamental parameters.

This means impeccable Italian, absence of grammatical errors, absolute respect for the guidelines. Citing numerical and factual data in an informative post, perhaps in the sector in which your company operates, and then specifying the reason why it is worth buying what you sell, is most often a successful strategy.

For example, did a travel agency hire you to promote a last-minute package? As a good copywriter, you need to be able to write down a highly emotional post that makes readers want to visit that particular tourist destination, solving all the problems associated with a vacation, such as stress in preparing and managing the available budget.

Knowing how to write to see means being able to intercept the target your company is targeting.

And, especially on the internet (e-mail marketing, review, landing page), but also in the press and in commercial letters, a high-impact title intrigues the reader, capturing their attention. Getting the title wrong is an inadmissible mistake for a copywriter since not attracting the interest of the reader is synonymous with loss of money for the company. Investing in the title is one of the challenges that the seller copywriter must succeed in winning.

However, clickbait should be avoided to the fullest. What is it? For many it is the worst of the web, that is to say, sensationalist titles whose primary objective is to bring a large number of visitors to the website to dramatically increase the number of visits or, in the case of paid to write websites, clicks on banners.

Often phrases are intentionally adopted which suggest a totally different meaning from the content of the article. In the era of social networks, these click-capture baits are increasingly common.

And at least once, let's face it, everyone took the bait. Using this copywriting technique is a sensational own goal, because the reader, after rolling his eyes and becoming so curious to read the content, is disappointed. Beaker marketing focused on the rule that a higher number of clicks corresponds to high earnings. Leveraging on the emotional aspect of the reader, first of all, anger and sadness, often completely false contents are spread in the online universe: fakes or better internet hoaxes.

Product Features

Creative writing that respects itself must highlight, almost in a hammering way, what are the real benefits of the product you are marketing.

This means that the product's strengths should not be presented as a shopping list. This would bore the reader and would be counterproductive in commercial terms. Potential customers almost have to touch the distinctive features of the product. And the words of the copywriter prove to be decisive. As an entrepreneur, not considering this means wasting time and wasting money.

Emotive Communication

Excessively verbose, cold, plastered, flat, inexpressive or pumped writing styles represent the death of the business. The reader gets bored and in terms of the image of your company he loses.

Writing to sell is the exact opposite because it means involving the reader and making them dream, stimulating their emotions. In practice, explain to the reader that the product that your company has put on the market is the top. You can intercept buyer people only if you know how to involve them. And this is feasible if they are at the center of your copywriting project. Creating a narrative capable of awakening a known need in the target, but interpreted in a new light is certainly a successful strategy.

How to implement it? By providing the essential information, the real benefits of the product immediately, but only some of the details. The secret lies in not being complete: buyers are keen to discover the rest of the article independently.

Knowing how to leave shaded areas is also an art.

Many of the readers intend to understand how to reach the conclusion and, despite your persuasive style, you go to accompany them in the shadow, the latter prefer to discover independently what is the path that leads them to the real benefit. What they need.

On social networks, then, the word artist must know how to create engagement, touch the emotional side of the members of the company page.

The crucial role of storytelling

The art of being able to tell stories, able to perfectly communicate what your company values are, is very important to attract new customers. Words are decisive, but also the spectacular nature of a video shot and the power of images (if you say that a picture is worth a thousand words, there is more than a concrete motivation) they are excellent allies of good writing. The more the mix has a high emotional impact, the more the content is in line with the value of the product and the identity of the company, the more success and sales will be high level. The final result of the narration must in any case always be original, in order to make the story unique and different from the others.

Clarity of words

The copywriter you hire to bring important numbers to sales must have a requirement that is a "conditio sine qua non": use a clear writing style, yes with a specific vocabulary but perfectly able to reach their destination even at the often mentioned Voghera housewife. Business jargon is not for everyone. Ditto for the marketese. The clarity of words and texts is the simplest way to transmit messages that arrive at their destination and that, consequently, are understood by the target to which your company addresses. The important thing, however, is that the words you use perhaps for the presentation of a product, shine within the text, capturing the attention of the end-user.

Watch the numbers!

The skilled copywriter, especially in informative or descriptive texts, in commercial communications, cannot fail to mention numbers.

Oh yes, because the numerical data are always counted.

Insert in an article the number of customers who have purchased the product, the high percentage of consumers who are reputed to be very satisfied or simply satisfied with the article they have won ... just what your company has put on the market, so to speak, it is extremely important.

Why? The numbers are always proof of the facts, they increase the level of conviction of those potential customers who are still a little undecided whether to make the purchase or to turn to the competition.

Moreover, the numbers make the work of copywriting even more concrete and testify to the previous reputation of your business reality. In short, numbers increase in order to increase sales.

A personal and identifying writing style

When a successful business copywriter writes a review, a post, a slogan, the contents of a website's homepage or landing page must always be original in content, almost creating, it must be said, a personal style in terms of communication. As an entrepreneur, he also considers this aspect, when you work with sales-oriented writing professional. If readers immediately identify the authoritativeness of the writer, your product can only benefit from it in terms of sales results. In the advertising field, for example, word games, like those rhymes and those unexpected assonances, have always been the history of advertising. And they will always continue to do so because they like them, they leave a smile on the lips of the reader or of those who listen to that slogan. Finally, they create buzz around the content, capturing the attention of the target.

Collection of testimonials

A sales-oriented writing style cannot do without testimonials. They must be easily identified by the reader: this means that name, surname, years, profession, city are data that must be present. Better if you also use a photo of them. After that, those who have tested the product put on the market must feel free to describe their user experience. The use of the first person with a lot of quotation marks proves to be a decisive lever to attract new customers and to boost the business volume of your company. Ultimately, in the texts created to increase sales, leaving the right space for the testimonials is one of the most effective strategies there is, since to be involved are persuasive factors that make inroads among the readers. The final message must in no way appear as an imposition, but on the contrary as advice that your best friend would give you.

The positive feedback of those who have already tested the product, especially on the Net, is fundamental. And word of mouth is confirmed as the quintessential advertising to make inroads among consumers. The latter in fact trust much more than the opinions of other buyers rather than of any other company.

Transparency is an added value

In copywriting, the truth about the product being advertised must in no way be hidden. Likewise, you never need to go overboard with a single fact. Therefore, transparency is one of the fundamental cornerstones for the writer.

No lies, given that, especially in the internet age, it takes very little to share a negative review on a product. In the eyes of the entrepreneur who hires a copywriter with the intention of giving a boost to yours, always ask yourself the question

But would the copywriter buy my product? If the answer is yes, then collaboration is feasible. In support of a planned marketing strategy, lies in no way find space in any type of article.

Details are important

The texts are fundamental to attract readers and, consequently, the target you approach. However, these alone are not enough. As in any work, the details are important and in the field of sales-oriented writing, the care of the graphics must be almost maniacal.

What do we mean to tell you? Simply that the chosen layout, both online and offline, must be clean and give a significant visual impact to the contents.

There is no better graphics than another, but a graphic that has its strong point in functionality: consolidating the commercial message and making a concrete contribution to your business is what the graphics must reveal.

Summing up, the effectiveness in copywriting work is mainly measured by the number of sales and leads procured for your business. And on these results, whether you believe it or not, the graphics must be functional to your business goals.

The importance of a call to action

When the writer writes to see, the call to action in the web world is nowadays decisive. The reason? The reader is invited to take action to become an effective customer or a lead. Among the most widespread calls to action, there are of course the purchase of the product, the registration for a newsletter, the filling in of the fields of a form. The call to action must, therefore, be emotional and engaging. Only then will the desired effect be achieved.

The skilled communication professional must be proactive, anticipating all (or almost all) of the questions from the reader. The writer's sales arguments must, in fact, be accompanied by detailed explanations aimed at anticipating any objections of the reference target of your company. In the age of the web, an objection can be considered to all intents and purposes as a real mine. Well, it is not hyperbole to assert that those who review your product must be able to extricate themselves from this minefield, defusing all the bombs.

Result of this modus operandi? Readers will be reassured and you will benefit in terms of sales.

For example, you are presenting an online German course that has a 20% higher price than the competitions price.

Being proactive means anticipating the objection but how come there is this price increase.

As a valid architect of the text, it will be up to you to throw down the words, possibly in capital letters and in bold, on the reasons for which to spend more is convenient, because the teachers are perhaps all native speakers or because the learning method adopted is truly revolutionary. In short, because the game is worth the candle.

Be reachable

In sales-oriented writing, leads need to be able to get in touch with your business in the easiest and fastest way.

Neglecting this aspect is a blunder that a far-sighted copywriter can never do. Landing pages without a contact form are a sensational own goal because in most cases it involves the impossibility that the demand, represented by your target, meets with the offer (your company).

At best, those who browse online and come across a landing page, where there is no contact form, will be forced to exit the landing page, type in your company name on a search engine, to go to the homepage of your website, to move to the contact page and to write to it from there. Do you have any idea how the path to an error like this has become more tortuous? Inserting the contact form would have taken just one click.

Another own goal is to insert too many fields to fill in the form. With this strategy, the CTR does not rise.

Simply enter the number of essential information. For the rest, there is a telephone.

Payment method and order management

In the e-commerce era, there is some information that needs to be clear right away.

Among these, the payment method and the order management (ie shipping) are among the most important. The potential customer, once he has decided to purchase the product on the website of your company, asks himself how he can pay and when he will receive the product.

Here, in a well-structured copywriting work the aforementioned information must be easily identifiable and immediately transparent.

Are there any additional costs for shipping? Should they be spun off? Is the cash on delivery not accepted as a payment method?

The thing must be clear upstream. Do you deliver to some countries? Very well.
But everything must be put on paper. What happens if the courier does not find the customer at home when the order is delivered? Your policy must be indicated

immediately. And if the product arrives defective at the destination? Or if the package arrives damaged at the address indicated by the buyer? In a sales-oriented writing job, these aspects must be specified and must be clear. In the event of any problems that depend on third parties, your company can avoid having a negative image, if everything is set down in black and white. The good copywriter must be able to translate all this into written words.

Conclusions

The aforementioned measures are valid for every type of sales communication, naturally making the necessary adjustments in relation to the specific product to be presented and the sales channel used, such as a newsletter, a page of your e-commerce site, a landing page, a brochure and so on. In short, the product changes, the channel changes, but the sales rules remain roughly the same.

In your copywriting works, always write texts that can awaken the emotions of those who read you. Use simple and fresh words that allow readers to understand how to meet their needs. And if they have none, they will begin to believe they have them because of your content. It is up to the words you will use to transport the target to which the company communicates towards the concrete benefits they will enjoy when they use the product you reviewed.

The simple characteristics of the products mentioned by way of simple list are too objective, cold and lacking in emotion. The classic bulleted list that knows a lot about the shopping list keeps people away from the purchase. As a professional in the field of content writing, it's up to you to turn features into advantages that are subjective, full of warmth and have the advantage of bringing the recipients of the message closer to the purchase.

Therefore, always focus on the contents, always devising them in relation to who the buyer personas are. Communicating in a persuasive, engaging, emotional and sincere way will get you better results from time to time. You will see that the efforts made in the field will give you great satisfaction!

Disclaimer

All registered trademarks and logos mentioned in this book belong to their respective owners.

The author of this book does not claim or declare any rights to these trademarks, which are mentioned only for educational and informational purposes.